African
Grasslands

Focus: Habitats

Meredith Costain

This book is about grasslands in Africa. Grasslands are places where the land is covered with grass.

Not many trees or bushes grow on grasslands.
There is not much shade.
There is not much shelter.

African grasslands
have two seasons.
Part of the year it is wet.
Part of the year it is dry.

The wet season is rainy.
The grass grows when
it rains.
The dry season is hot.
Then the grass gets stiff
and brown.

Many animals find food
on the African grasslands.
Birds eat the seeds
that the grass makes.

Zebras eat the grass.

Cheetahs are predators.
Predators hunt other animals.

Hyenas are predators, too. But sometimes hyenas eat meat that other animals leave behind.

Animals that eat grass
find ways to be safe
from predators.
Impalas live in groups.
Animals in groups
can protect others.

Wildebeests are very fast runners.
Fast runners can outrun predators.

Giraffes live in groups
like impalas.
They are very fast runners
like wildebeests.

Rabbits have fur the color of dry grass.
Their fur helps hide them from predators.

Meerkats live in burrows under the grasslands. Their burrows help hide them from predators.

People share the
grasslands, too.
They make small homes
and use the grasses
to make food.

Index

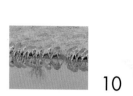